Democracy

Democracy in Australia

Pearson Australia
(a division of Pearson Australia Group Pty Ltd)
707 Collins Street, Melbourne, Victoria 3008
PO Box 23360, Melbourne, Victoria 8012
www.pearson.com.au

First published 2011 by Pearson Australia
2018 2017 2016
10 9 8 7 6 5 4

Authors: Cameron Macintosh and Carmel Reilly
Publisher: Sarah Russell
Project Editor: Rachel Davis
Editor: Writers Reign
Designers: Anne Donald, Jan Urbanic and Kim Ferguson
Cover Designer: Glen McClay
Copyright & Pictures Editor: Katy Murenu
Printed in Australia by the SOS Print + Media Group

National Library of Australia Cataloguing-in-Publication entry
Author: Macintosh, Cameron.
Title: Democracy in Australia / Cameron Macintosh and Carmel Reilly.
ISBN: 9781442559684 (pbk.)
Series: Democracy.
Notes: Includes index.
Target Audience: For primary school age.
Subjects: Democracy--Australia--Juvenile literature.
Democracy--Australia--History.
Other Authors/Contributors: Reilly, Carmel.
Dewey Number: 321.80994

Pearson Australia Group Pty Ltd ABN 40 004 245 943

Acknowledgements
We would like to thank the following for permission to reproduce copyright material.
The following abbreviations are used in this list: t = top, b = bottom, r = right.

AAP: Dean Lewins, p. 17; David Moore, p. 28; Gary Ramage, p. 27b.
Australian Electoral Commission: p. 15b.
Battye Library, State Library of Western Australia: p. 11b.
Corbis: Andrew Gombert, p. 19; Richard Hutchings, p. 5t.
Fairfax Photo Sales: p. 20; John French, p. 15br; Jim McEwen, p. 21; Russel McPhedran, p. 23.
Getty Images: pp. 13, 15t, 26, 25; Paula Bronstein, p. 27t; Pedro Costa, p. 29.
National Archives of Australia: p. 11t.
National Library of Australia: pp. 22t, 22b.
Newspix: p. 18; Richard Gosling, p. 5b.
Public Records Office, Victoria: p. 8.
Shutterstock: cover.
State Library of NSW: Mitchell Library a12811, p. 6; Dixson Galleries a2828001, p. 7; Dixson Galleries a928710, p. 9.

Every effort has been made to trace and acknowledge copyright. However, if any infringement has occurred, the publishers tender their apologies and invite the copyright holders to contact them.

Some of the images used in *Democracy in Australia* might have associations with deceased Indigenous Australians. Please be aware that these images might cause sadness or distress in Aboriginal or Torres Strait Islander communities.

Contents

Words that are printed in bold are explained in the Glossary on page 31.

What Is Democracy?

Democracy is a way of making group decisions that allows everyone in the group to have a say. It is a system that tries to work out what is best for the whole group while keeping in mind the rights of the individuals within it. The word 'democracy' comes from the ancient Greeks and it means the 'rule of the people' or 'majority rule'. Abraham Lincoln, the 16th president of the United States, described democracy as 'government of the people, by the people, for the people'.

Democracy: Key Beliefs

- Individuals within a group are equal and no one is better or has a higher value than anyone else.
- The things that happen to a group affect all its members.
- The best decisions for a group are those that everyone has discussed and understood.
- Every individual within a group needs to feel safe and be protected.

Forms of Democracy

There are two main forms of democracy—direct democracy and indirect democracy.

Direct Democracy

In a direct democracy, people can have a say in decision-making by voicing their opinions or voting directly on any issues that might affect them. Direct democracy works best in small groups and communities where it is easy for everyone to get information or to voice an opinion. In larger communities, this becomes too difficult. There are often hundreds of issues that need to be discussed, and it is impossible for each person to know enough about every issue to make an informed decision.

Indirect Democracy

In an indirect democracy, commonly called a **representative** democracy, certain people are **elected** by members of the community to represent them in an **assembly** or **parliament**. These representatives make decisions on behalf of the people who voted for them. Because of their size, modern democratic nations are nearly always representative democracies.

Protecting Democracy

In order for a democracy to be truly representative, it is important to ensure that there are safeguards to stop the government from becoming too powerful, and to guarantee that people's rights and freedoms are protected. Some of the safeguards in a representative democracy include a written **constitution**, fair laws that can be upheld by an independent legal system, freedom of speech, a free media and access to government information.

About This Book

This book looks at democracy in Australia, including how the Australian democracy came into being, the types of electoral systems that have been chosen, and the sorts of safeguards that have been put in place to make sure that government is as representative as possible. This book also focuses on democracy in action in Australia, including the rights and responsibilities of **citizens** and the role that government and pressure groups play to ensure that society remains fair.

These students are voting for a class leader, which shows democracy in action.

These workers are meeting to discuss improving their work conditions, which shows democracy in action.

From Colony to Nation

The first European settlement in Australia was established at Port Jackson in Sydney in 1788. The first settlers were convicts, sent by the British Government to serve their sentences in the new British colony of New South Wales.

Early Years

In the first years of settlement, the convicts faced famine and sometimes violent resistance from the local **Indigenous** people. Government and the society in the new settlement were often in chaos. But the settlement survived and the British Government sent more convicts. With the arrival of free settlers, the population began to swell. By 1800, there were about 5000 Europeans living in New South Wales. By 1820, this number had grown to 26 000.

Steps Towards Democracy in Australia

The first fleet of convicts and soldiers sent to New South Wales was commanded by Captain Arthur Phillip. He became the governor of the colony and established the first settlement at Port Jackson. He governed single-handedly in the name of the British **monarch**, and had complete power, including being able to pass the death sentence on those who disobeyed his commands.

After Phillip returned to England in 1792, a series of governors was sent to run the colony. By the early 1820s, there were complaints from some of the colonists that the governor had too much power. To help address this problem, the British Government established a Legislative Council to help the governor run the colony in 1823.

From One Colony to Six

With increased migration, other colonies were established. The first was Van Diemen's Land (Tasmania) in 1825, followed by Western Australia in 1829, South Australia in 1836, Victoria in 1851 and Queensland in 1859. Many people living in the colonies started to believe that they should have a right to elect their own governments.

The first local elections for the Legislative Council of New South Wales were held in 1843, although only wealthy men were **eligible** to vote. By 1851, elections were held in South Australia, Tasmania and Victoria and, in 1855, these states also adopted **constitutions**. In the same year, Victoria became the first state to grant **universal suffrage** for men.

Captain Arthur Phillip raised the British flag when the First Fleet landed on Australian soil.

Captain Arthur Phillip commanded the First Fleet and became the first governor of the colony of New South Wales.

Legislative Council of New South Wales

At first, the council consisted of between five and seven members and had little power. Not only were members **appointed** by the governor, but the governor always had final say on any matter. In 1828, the council was expanded to between 10 and 15 members, who were able to make decisions based on the majority of votes and could override the governor.

Journey to Federation

In 1888, 100 years after the first European settlement, seven out of every 10 people who lived in the Australian colonies had been born there. Most of these people found it hard to accept government by a power on the other side of the world. While there were many differences between the colonies, there were many things they shared, and for some people, **federation**, or combining of the colonies into one nation, made a lot of sense.

Reasons to Unite

The idea of federation began to be taken more seriously in 1883 when two large foreign powers, France and Germany, established colonies in the Pacific. Many people were fearful that the Australian colonies could be invaded by one of these powers. They thought that the colonies would have a better chance of protecting themselves if they were united and could form a stronger defence force.

Other factors that made people think more about federation were transport and **tariffs**. Because the colonies had different rail systems, every time goods crossed borders they had to change trains. Each colony also put tariffs on goods as they crossed borders. This was expensive for individuals and confusing to manage, because each colony charged different rates—even for the same goods.

Opposition

Despite this, many people were against federation. Those in the smaller colonies feared that New South Wales and Victoria would control a federated nation. There was also a lot of rivalry between New South Wales and Victoria, and neither trusted the other not to take over. Furthermore, many Australians lived in remote parts of the country and did not feel connected to other areas—federation was simply not important to them.

Promoting the Idea

As time went on, it became obvious that the colonies had to work together. Tariffs were seen as a barrier to healthy trade. At the same time, better transport and communication would make more people feel part of the wider Australian community.

A small group of individuals began to promote the idea of a federated Australia. Men such as Sir Henry Parkes, Alfred Deakin and Edmund Barton changed the minds of many Australians about federation. They also worked out how federation could be achieved by putting forward a **constitution** to lead the new country into the 20th century.

Prior to Federation, trains travelled on different types of tracks in each colony and had to offload their cargo at colony borders.

Sir Henry Parkes

Sir Henry Parkes (1815–96) served as premier of New South Wales three times between 1872 and 1891. He was a vocal promoter of federation for almost 50 years. He was behind many of the federation conferences, including the 1890 federation conference, which marked the turning point in the acceptance of a united Australia.

Creating a Constitution

National Australasian Convention

In March 1891, **delegates** met in Sydney at the National Australasian Convention to find common ground about **federation**. Sir Henry Parkes, who was elected president of the convention, presented a number of proposals to the group, including the structure of a national government that would oversee the running of the whole country. This government's responsibilities would include the **armed forces**, transport and communication. According to this plan, the colonies would become states and remain in charge of their own areas and laws.

After six weeks of discussion by delegates, a draft framework for the Australian **constitution** was written. It provided a structure for the government with a **bicameral parliament**, made up of a lower house (House of Representatives) and an upper house (Senate). While the number of seats in the House of Representatives was based on population, the Senate would have an equal number of representatives from each state, regardless of size. This would help to protect the interests of states with small populations.

What Is a Constitution?

A constitution sets out the way in which a country is governed. It outlines the structure and organisation of the government, its powers, the laws it can make, and the way the court system is run. Some constitutions also contain a Bill of Rights stating the rights of the nation's citizens.

Taking It to the People

For the next 10 years, a number of men, including Edmund Barton and George Reid from New South Wales, Alfred Deakin from Victoria and Sir Samuel Griffith from Queensland, dedicated their lives to the movement. They travelled across the continent, putting their ideas across to as many people as possible. After Federation, Barton was to become the first prime minister of Australia, while Deakin would become the second.

More conferences followed, including a 'people's conference' held at Corowa, Victoria, in 1893. There, a motion was passed that delegates to further conferences on federation should be elected by the people of each state. Another motion proposed that **referendums** be held in each colony so that the people could choose directly to become a part of federated Australia. At a conference in Bathurst, New South Wales, in 1896, representatives were chosen who would, supposedly, represent every class and as many different interest groups as possible.

Between 1897 and 1898, one last convention to finalise the constitution was held in Adelaide, Sydney and Melbourne. After all the points were finally accepted, the constitution was ready to be put before the people to approve in a referendum. In 1899, following two referendums, the people of the colonies, apart from Western Australia, agreed to federate. A year later, Western Australia also voted to join the new nation.

Sir Henry Parkes (seated, middle) poses for a photo with other delegates at the National Australasian Convention in 1891.

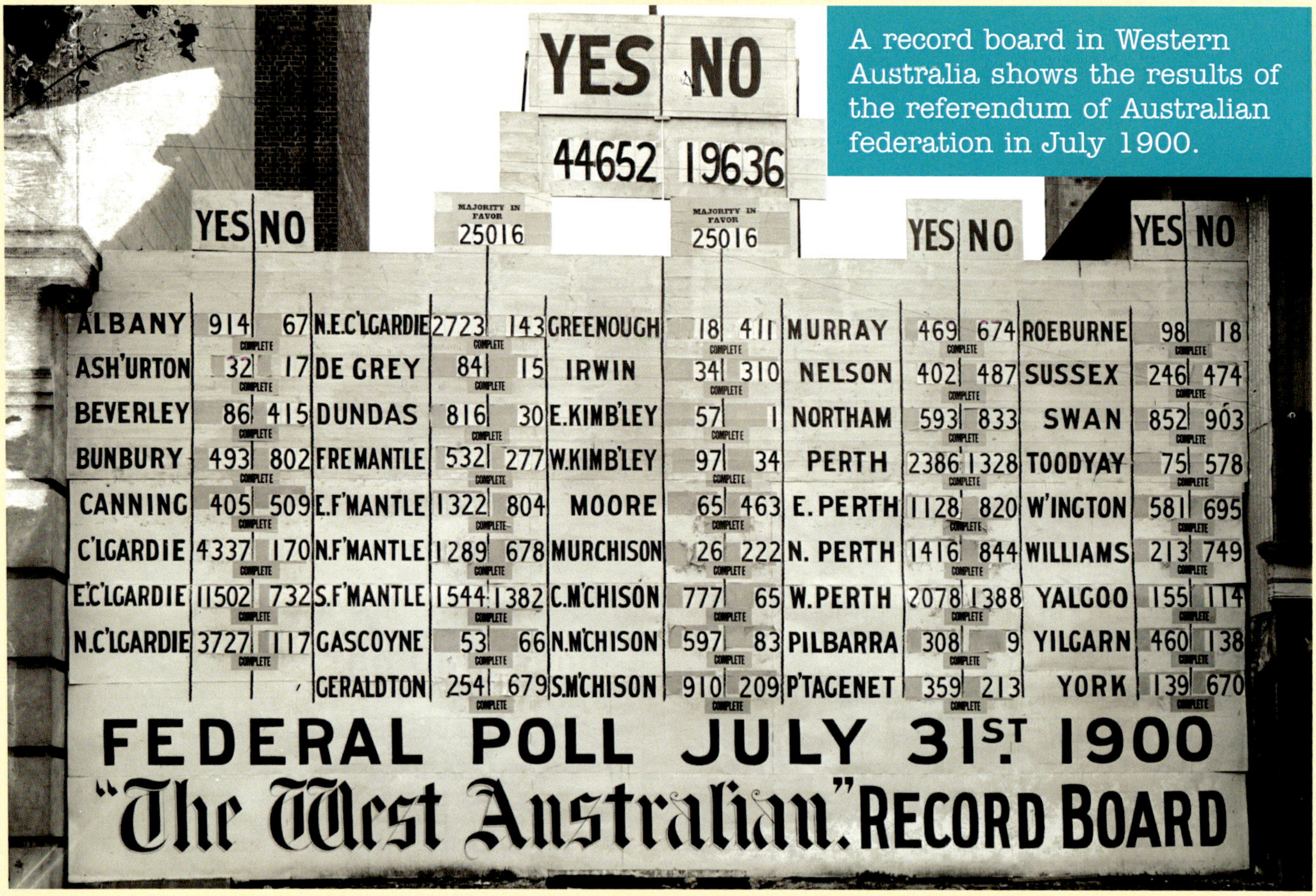

A record board in Western Australia shows the results of the referendum of Australian federation in July 1900.

Government in Australia

Australia has three levels of government: federal, state and local. The federal government is responsible for areas such as defence, trade, taxes and foreign relations. The states and territories have their own governments that are responsible for schools, hospitals, police and ambulance services, housing and transport. Local governments run smaller areas and take care of parks and gardens, rubbish removal and planning.

Federal Government

The Australian **constitution** sets up a **bicameral** federal **parliament** made up of a House of Representatives and a Senate. The government is divided into three branches: the **executive**, which runs the country; the **legislature**, which makes the laws that govern the country; and the **judiciary**, which enforces and interprets the laws.

Structure of Federal Government

Executive

- The British monarch is the head of state in Australia. His or her role is **ceremonial**.
- The Governor-General acts as the head of state for the monarch but has little real power. The Governor-General assents (agrees) to **legislation** after it has been passed by both houses of parliament.
- The prime minister is head of government and the leader of **cabinet**. He or she is always a member of the House of Representatives.
- Cabinet is made up of the government's most important **ministers**. Cabinet helps the prime minister decide on policies.
- Government departments put laws and policy into action. Each department is headed by a minister.

Legislature

- The Australian Parliament has two houses: the House of Representatives and the Senate. The House of Representatives has 150 members. The Senate has 76 members.

Judiciary

- The judiciary includes the High Court that deals with constitutional issues and is also a court of appeal. Below that is the Federal Court, which deals with matters to do with federal government laws and native title; and the Family Court that deals with divorce and child custody. A federal magistrate's court hears less complex cases to do with federal law or families.

State, Territory and Local Governments

State and territory governments deal with issues and services to do with their areas. Like the federal government, they have three branches. The states each have a governor who acts as a largely symbolic head of state, as well as their own constitutions, while the territories refer to the Governor-General and the federal constitution.

Local governments provide services to local areas. They have elected councillors who steer the direction of the council, while paid employees deliver services.

HOUSE OF REPRESENTATIVES SEATING PLAN

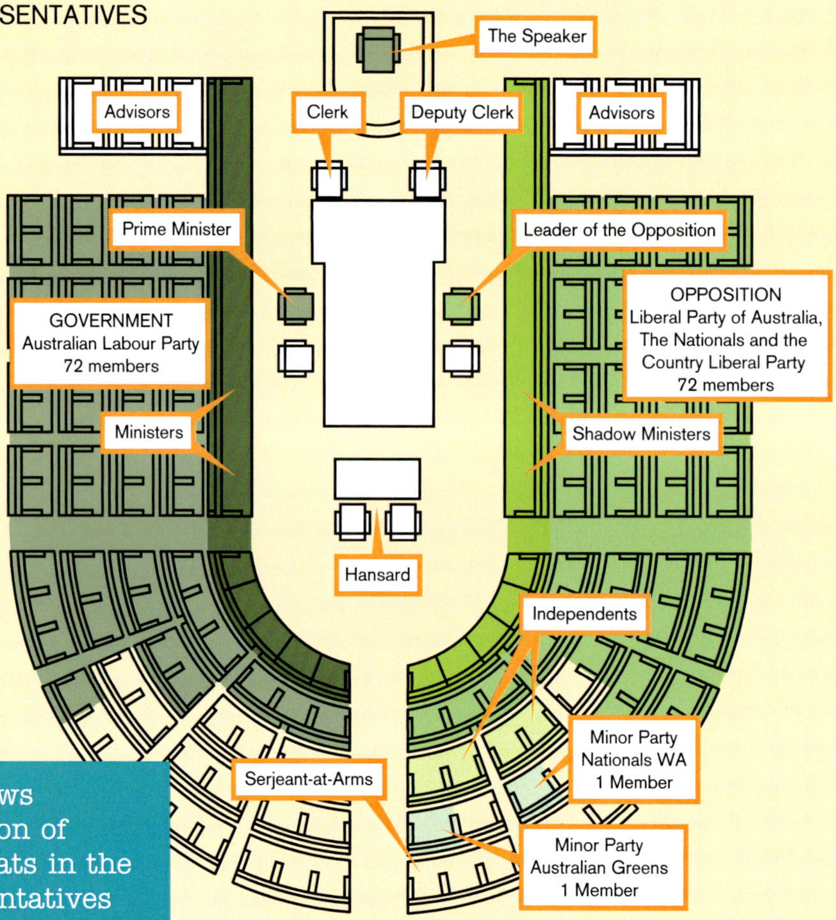

This diagram shows the party allocation of parliamentary seats in the House of Representatives in 2011.

Australia's federal parliament meets at Parliament House in Canberra. This picture shows the Australian House of Representatives.

Choosing Representatives

In an election, there should be a wide range of **candidates** and parties for voters to choose from; and all adult citizens should be **eligible** to vote, regardless of race, gender or beliefs. When Australia became a nation in 1901, only white males were allowed to vote. **Suffrage** was granted to women in 1902, but Indigenous people were not granted that right in federal elections until 1962.

Elections

In Australia today, with a few exceptions, it is compulsory for citizens over the age of 18 to vote. When they do, there are a variety of **political** parties and independent candidates for them to choose from. Federal elections are held every three years, and most state elections and local government elections are held every four years.

Electorates and Seats

Each member of the House of Representatives represents an area called an **electorate**, which contains on average 94 000 people. These representatives hold a **seat** in parliament.

Different Voting Systems

In federal elections, the House of Representatives is elected using the **preferential voting** system. In this system, voters put numbers beside each candidate in the order of preference, starting with 1 beside the candidate they most want. A candidate who wins more than 50 per cent of the 1 votes will win. If this does not happen, the candidate with the least 1 votes is eliminated and their number 2 votes are given to the other candidates. This process continues until someone gains more than 50 per cent of the votes.

Voting for the Senate is done by **proportional representation**. Again, voters put preference numbers next to the candidates' names. The numbers are worked out on percentages and the candidates who get the most 1s are given the seats that are available. Similar voting systems are used by state and local governments throughout Australia.

Political Parties

The first political party in Australia was the Australian Labor Party (ALP), which was formed in 1890 to protect the rights of workers. Another important party in Australia, the Liberal Party, was formed in 1944 as a supporter of business and free enterprise. At times, to help win government, the Liberal Party has formed a **coalition** with the National Party, a party that looks after the interests of farmers. Since the 1920s, these three parties have controlled government.

Some smaller parties, such as the Australian Greens, which focus on social and environmental issues, have also gained seats in parliament, mostly in the Senate. Smaller parties sometimes hold the **balance of power** in the Senate, which means they are able to stop laws being passed by the Senate if they do not agree with them.

Former Prime Minister John Howard (third from left) with cabinet ministers, January 2007.

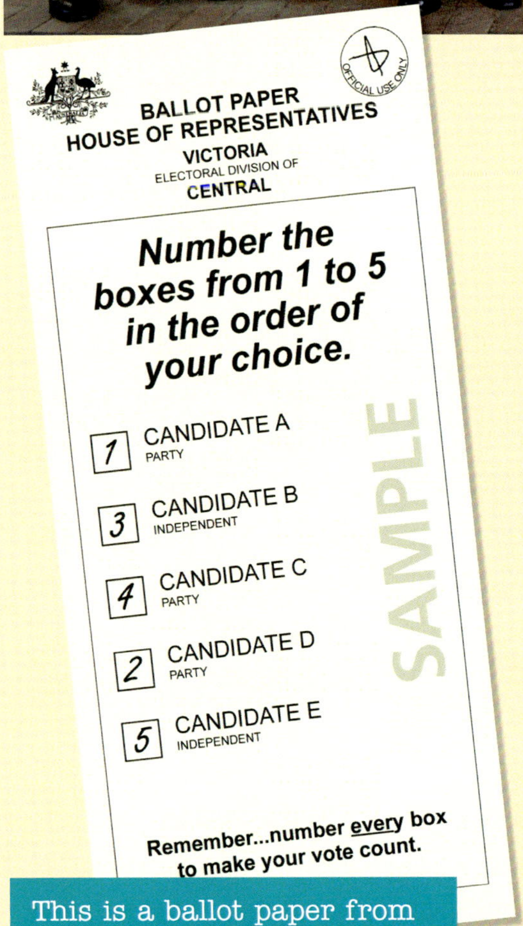

BALLOT PAPER
HOUSE OF REPRESENTATIVES
VICTORIA
ELECTORAL DIVISION OF
CENTRAL

OFFICIAL USE ONLY

Number the boxes from 1 to 5 in the order of your choice.

1	CANDIDATE A PARTY
3	CANDIDATE B INDEPENDENT
4	CANDIDATE C PARTY
2	CANDIDATE D PARTY
5	CANDIDATE E INDEPENDENT

SAMPLE

Remember...number every box to make your vote count.

This is a ballot paper from an Australian election.

Politicans at the Constitutional Convention at Old Parliament House in Canberra ready to hand in their ballot papers, 13 February 1998.

Democracy in Action

Democracy is built on the belief that people have certain rights and freedoms. Some of these include the right of free expression, of free **assembly** and of **association**. These rights and freedoms ensure that people can say what they want, to whomever they want, and join with others to form protest or pressure groups if and when needed. Rights also include the right to choose a representative government, to access information about what that government does, and to pass judgement on that government's policies and actions.

Rights and Responsibilities

People who are a part of a democracy expect to have their rights upheld. However, in order to have rights, people also have responsibilities. A large part of being in a democracy is about compromise, including learning to live with others and going along with decisions that have been made by the majority of the population. But this does not mean that **citizens** have no choice. If they feel strongly about an issue, citizens also have a responsibility to voice their opinions, either by approaching the government or by **lobbying** or peaceful protest.

Role of Government

There are many ways that democratic governments themselves can protect and further citizens' rights. In Australia, these include a written **constitution** that outlines the form and structure of the government, and an effective court system that can check the laws that the government has made. In a democracy, elected **representatives** should be working on behalf of the citizens who voted for them, and this means making laws that are good for the community.

Missing Bill of Rights

Many people have criticised Australia's constitution because, unlike constitutions in most other democracies, it does not include a Bill of Rights. A Bill of Rights sets out political rights, like freedom of speech, as well as **social** rights, such as the right to healthcare and education.

Those who support the present constitution say a Bill of Rights is not necessary because people's rights are protected by the parliamentary system, which creates laws on behalf of its citizens, and the **judiciary**, which can uphold or reject these laws.

Others argue that a Bill of Rights is important in a constitution because people's rights are at the heart of democracy and, if they are not clearly laid out, they could easily be ignored. Laws can take a long time to be made; sometimes, they may never be made. The Australian Constitution was written at a time when many of the human rights taken for granted today were not considered important. Many people feel it needs to be updated.

Thousands of people joined an Occupy Sydney protest march in Sydney, 5 November 2011.

Other Voices in Democracy

Media

The media—newspapers, magazines, radio, television and the internet—plays an important role in a democratic society. It helps citizens make choices about the **candidates** and parties that stand for election, and also helps them to assess how their government is performing. In order to be able to fulfil this function, it is important to have a free media, that is, a media that can put forward a variety of viewpoints or criticise the actions of the government.

While the media in Australia is free to say what it wants, in recent times it has been criticised for not being diverse enough—that is, having too few owners, and therefore not expressing a wide enough range of opinions. This means that if the owner has a particular **political** viewpoint, it could well be reflected in many publications and not just one or two. Many people now look to the internet as a source of information because it reflects a variety of points of view.

Interest Groups

Special interest groups seek to educate and influence both the government and the public. The labour movement and the environmental movement are just two of many groups that play a major part in Australian political life.

- Labour Movement

  The labour movement is a term for groups that **campaign** for better conditions and pay for workers. Trade unions are one of the most visible parts of the labour movement. The first organised Australian trade unions were set up in the 1830s. However, since the beginning of European settlement in Australia, many individuals and groups have protested about unfair working conditions.

Birth of the ALP

In the late 1800s, a strike by shearers for better pay and conditions led to unions from all around the country striking. General strikes brought many parts of Australia to a standstill and led to the colonial governments calling troops to put an end to the disruptions. The governments then created laws that made it difficult for people to join unions. Out of the conflict of this period, the pro-union Australian Labor Party was born. By 1914, it held government in every state.

- Environmental Movement

  Perhaps no other cause has had as much exposure in the last 30 years as the environmental movement. Individuals and organisations have **lobbied** the government and protested against the damming of the Franklin River in Tasmania, the wood chipping of native forests, and uranium mining and export. In 1992, the Australian Greens formed a national political party. By 2011, they had gained nine seats in the Senate and their first member in the House of Representatives.

Bob Brown, leader of the Australian Greens party and actor Lorraine Bayly, led the protest against the damming of the Franklin River in the early 1980s.

Prime Minister Julia Gillard faces questions from the media at a 2011 press conference.

Indigenous Australians

Indigenous Australians are thought to have first arrived on the continent between 50 000 and 60 000 years ago. Their way of living was tribal. Decision-making was usually done by councils of elders, according to strict law and custom. Indigenous people did not believe land could be owned by individuals; instead, they thought of it as a part of themselves. When the new settlers forced them away from their traditional lands, their grief was overwhelming. The Europeans brought not only misery but also death to Indigenous people, mostly from disease and malnutrition (due to loss of land and hunting grounds). The Indigenous population dropped from more than 500 000 at first contact to about 30 000 by the end of the 1800s.

After Colonisation

Many Indigenous people who survived were taken to government or religious institutions, where they were trained to become workers for white people and expected to fit into white society. Families were separated, and children were taken from their parents.

Many Indigenous children were removed from their families and forced to fit into white society.

Life in the 21st Century

Indigenous people were granted full voting rights in 1962 and were finally granted full **citizenship** in 1967. Despite these changes, life for most Indigenous people did not improve. At the beginning of the 21st century, life expectancy for Indigenous people was 20 years below European life expectancy, and housing and education standards in many communities were vastly lower.

Land Rights

For more than 100 years, calls for Indigenous land rights were ignored. However, in 1982, Eddie Mabo from the Island of Mer in the Torres Strait put up a legal challenge against the Queensland Government on behalf of his people. In 1992, the High Court ruled that the people of Mer owned their land because they could prove that they had always lived on it.

This case was a turning point for Indigenous land rights because the High Court recognised that since 1788 Indigenous people had wrongfully been denied rights to their land. However, the law only recognises ownership of people who have continuously lived on their land. Many groups who have left or been removed from their lands have been unable to make claims.

Eddie Mabo, from the Torres Strait island of Mer, led the fight for Indigenous ownership of traditional lands to be recognised by the courts.

The Stolen Generation

The practice of taking Aboriginal children from their families 'for their own good' and having them adopted by white families was common in Australia well into the 20th century. The victims of this practice are known as the Stolen Generation. In 2008, Prime Minister Kevin Rudd apologised to members of the Stolen Generation on behalf of the government and people of Australia for the suffering that they, their families and their communities have experienced.

Women in Australia

In 1902, Australia became one of the first countries in the world to give women the vote and to allow women to stand as **candidates** for election. Despite gaining this right, it took some time for women to be elected to **parliament**. The first woman elected to a state parliament was Edith Cowan in Western Australia in 1921, but it was not until 1943 that Dame Enid Lyons and Dame Dorothy Tangney were elected to federal parliament.

Louisa Lawson

Louisa Lawson (1848–1920) was a **feminist** and a **suffragette**. She ran and edited a pro-**federation** newspaper called *Republican*, before starting a feminist magazine called *Dawn*. This magazine supported issues such as women's education and the right to vote. In 1889, she founded the Dawn Club, which became the centre for women's **suffrage** in Sydney.

Vida Goldstein

Vida Goldstein (1869–1949) from Victoria became the first woman in Australia to stand for election in the federal election of 1903. Although she was unsuccessful, she continued to stand for parliament in elections until 1917. Throughout her life, she campaigned for suffrage and equal property rights for men and women.

20th Century

Although women could vote and stand for parliament, for most of the 20th century only small numbers of women were elected. Women still lacked the same rights as men in other areas. They did not receive equal pay for equal work and were unable to work in certain jobs. Women were not protected by the law against sexual harassment or violence in the home, and it was difficult for them to go to university. Banks would not lend money to women who were single.

In the 1960s, many of these issues began to be recognised and discussed. The Women's Electoral Lobby (WEL) was established in 1972, with the idea of informing women about the best party for them in the federal election. Soon, WEL had expanded into research and **activism** on a range of women's issues. WEL and other groups and individuals brought pressure on governments to change laws and create facilities for women. These included health clinics, child-care centres, and refuges for women and children who had suffered family violence. In 1974, the law was changed to allow women equal pay for equal work.

21st Century

By 2010, the number of women in parliament had grown from two in 1943 to a total of 67 in 2010, with women making up 25 per cent of the House of Representatives and 39 per cent of the Senate. Today, women make up larger numbers of students in higher education and are free to take up any kind of job. However, on average, their incomes are still about 17 per cent lower than those of men.

Germaine Greer, a campaigner for Women's Rights, leads a demonstration in Sydney in 1972.

Looking to the Future

As Australians look to the future, one of the issues they have been discussing is the idea of Australia becoming a **republic**. In a republic, the head of state is a president who is either directly elected by the people, or indirectly elected by members of **parliament**. The head of state represents the country, but does not usually represent the government.

Republic Referendum

In 1999, after much public debate, the government held a **referendum** asking the Australian people if they wanted to change their **political** system from a **constitutional monarchy** to a republic. Fifty-four per cent of people voted against the idea.

Where to Next?

Many people believe that the question of a republic will return again. In 2004, a senate inquiry found that the referendum should be put before the Australian people again, as the last referendum was too complex. It not only asked people about a republic, but also suggested a particular way of voting for a president. This meant that while many people wanted a republic, they voted against the idea because they did not like the way of choosing a president that was offered to them.

The senate inquiry recommended that, before having another referendum, there should be a wide-reaching education program to teach people about the Australian **Constitution** and the different ways of setting up a republic. It also recommended that only one simple question should be asked: Do you want a republic in Australia? When this question is answered, the people of Australia can then go on to the next step.

Arguments For and Against a Republic

FOR

- The head of state in a republic is elected directly or indirectly by the people of that country. Australia should have a head of state that the people choose to represent their country.
- The Queen is not Australian and should not represent Australians as head of state.
- Many Australians do not have a British background and should not have a British **monarch** as their head of state.
- Many of the world's great democracies, such as the United States and France, are republics.
- Opinion polls show that most Australians want Australia to be a republic.

AGAINST

- The monarchy has worked well in the past and there is no reason why it will not continue to do so.
- The Queen is above politics. She does not favour any one party, while a president will most probably be a member of a party.
- Britain settled Australia and having a British monarch as head of state recognises this fact.
- Many other countries in the Asian region have monarchies, such as Japan, Thailand and Malaysia.

Queen Elizabeth II visited Australia in October 2011.

Local Versus Global

When Australia first became a nation in 1901, the world was a very different place. There was no radio, television or internet. There were no planes and a journey to Europe took about six weeks by ship. Most businesses were small and locally run. At **Federation**, people worried about giving up their local colonial identities to become part of a larger nation.

Fast forward 100 years and the scene is very different. Today, Australians are as much a part of a global community as they are a national community. News comes from all over the world, and thanks to global corporations, people in any country are able to listen to the same kind of music, wear the same kind of clothes or eat the same kind of food. This kind of **globalisation** does not just affect individuals and the way they see the world, it also affects governments and the way countries are run.

Government Decision-making

Today, there are many decisions that the government has to make based on forces outside Australia. Throughout the 20th century, most large corporations became global, employing more and more people around the world. Now there are hundreds of global corporations with offices and factories in Australia. When the government makes **economic** decisions, it has to keep these corporations in mind because they are a large part of the Australian economy and help to bring money into the country.

However, while supporting these companies may bring growth to the country, it may not always be good for Australian companies or employees. The government also has to make decisions about its defence and trade that are not always good for some parts of the Australian community, but benefit the country as a whole.

International Organisations

Australia, like most countries in the world, belongs to international organisations such as the United Nations (UN), the **International Monetary Fund** (IMF) and the World Trade Organization (WTO). The UN was founded at the end of World War II to help promote peace, security, human rights and social development. The IMF and the WTO were established to help with economic stability and trade around the world.

As a member of the UN, Australia has a commitment to world-wide human rights, trade and development. It is the 12th largest contributor to the UN's budget and provides forces for UN peace-keeping missions.

Australia in the G20

Australia is a member of the G20 (Group of Twenty), an international forum for economic cooperation. The G20 was established in 1999, with the aim of overcoming and preventing global financial crises.

Kevin Rudd, the Australian Foreign Minister, addresses a UN General Assembly in New York in 2010.

Over 1100 Australian United Nations peacekeepers work in East Timor, helping to restore democracy.

Global Connections

Fast travel and instant communication mean that Australians can be connected to countries thousands of kilometres away. The internet offers an easy way for people to become part of communities outside their countries. People band together online to play games and talk about anything from art to politics. Since the 1990s, the internet has also become a place where people can discuss and plan protests and actions. Meetings of the World Trade Organization, which many people believed supported undemocratic forms of **globalisation**, were disrupted many times by protesters who had organised rallies on the internet. This included a rally in Melbourne in 2002.

Migration

In the 1950s, Australia opened up migration from non-English-speaking countries. It is now home to a diverse population with connections to people in every country in the world. The federal government adopted a policy of **multiculturalism** in the early 1970s, recognising that those who migrate have a right to keep their own cultures alive while at the same time becoming a part of Australian society. One of the challenges to democracy in Australia today is to keep these rights and responsibilities balanced.

What the Future Holds

Although there have been many changes in Australia over the last 100 years, the way the country is governed is still much the same. While some people are concerned that the Australian democracy may no longer be as strong because of global ties and the attitude of many people to politicians, others think it is alive and well. They point out that the rights of more of the population are recognised and accepted by law than they were a century ago, and that there are more groups openly protesting and expressing their concerns across a range of issues.

Issues for the future of Australian democracy include the growth of globalisation and the rise of technology, lack of privacy, and environmental and social concerns. In the end, the only way to ensure that these issues are addressed is for people to continue to take part in the democratic process by voting and joining community and pressure groups.

In the 1950s and 1960s, many migrants from non-English-speaking counties such as Italy and Greece arrived in Australia.